Brutal, Raw & Beautiful

Kitt Blessing

BookLeaf Publishing

India | USA | UK

Presentation by *BookLeaf Publishing*

Web: www.bookleafpub.com

E-mail: info@bookleafpub.com

ISBN: 9789363300507

First edition 2024

These pages wouldn't be

Possible without all of you

So thank you a ton

For all that you do:

Becca, Ann Marie, Karen,

Ruba, Sal, and Jen,

Mom, Dad, Pat, Uncles Lou, John, and my family,

Marvin and My Dude Tym,

My Girlfriend Melissa, Val, Jill, Nicole, Todd,

Ms. Odatalla and Mr. Williams too,

And of course, gentle Reader,

Many thanks are given to you too!

ACKNOWLEDGEMENT

Thanks to everyone who ever helped me along my journey, especially all of my teachers, mentors and friends.

To my nephews, always be yourselves, no matter what happens along the way. You are all rockstars.

Special Thanks to Melissa Wright for the photograph for the cover of this book.

Special Thanks to Tym Moss for, inadvertently, giving me the title of this book.

PREFACE

They say the path to self-discovery is a difficult one, and mine is no different. This is the story of my life, and more importantly, the story of figuring out, at thirty-seven years old, exactly who I am and who I am meant to be. It is a story that contains brutal, raw and beautiful moments that helped me discover and shape the person I am today–a person who, finally, after so many years, I am happy, proud, and free to be. And so, gentle reader, come with me now and enter into my world and experience the complex yet ultimately empowering journey into my transition from womanhood to manhood.

Finding the Hall of Memory

"Hey, listen up,
Open your eyes," a voice does say
"Take my hand,
Hurry, I know the way."

"But who are you?"
"I'm your spectral guide,
I'm here to help you find
And uncover what's deep inside."

"Are we going on a journey?"
"No, a very difficult quest,
So open your eyes and follow
Quickly, at my behest."

Reluctantly, I do so,
Unsure of what I'll see,
But much to my surprise
In a mirror, I'm looking at me.

The image is blurry
A bit unfocused too
"You'll understand why,
But I promise that image is you."

"But what is this?"
I ask to the air,
"Step through the glass,
Don't worry, I'll be there."

Hesitantly, I touch it,
As if in a dream
And then I pass through,
And fully intact, it does seem.

Suddenly a split path opens before me
One colorful, one dark,
A dichotomy of choices
On which to make my mark.

"What way do I go?"
I ask my unseen guide.
"Whatever way you wish
The answer just lies inside."

Light or dark
Dark or light
Which is the better way
Which is the lesser fight?

"You must choose soon,
As the portal will close
Let your feet decide
Your soul already knows."

I close my eyes
My feet turn towards the right
The shadows start to close
And turn into an endless night.

A struggle ahead
Too late to turn 'round
What horrors await
What treasures to be found?

I start traveling ahead,
Facing boldly the unknown
I just hope this path
Will eventually lead me home.

A Memory Unlocked

A memory appears
As I walk down the path
Distant and fuzzy
But one that seemed to last.

Child me is standing
Shaking in fear
A grey shirt clutched to her chest
Fury is near.

"I don't want to hear
Again this nonsense from you
God made you perfect
In who you are and all you do."

Child me starts to cry
The grey shirt ripped away
"God made you a girl
There's nothing left to say."

Child me's suddenly alone
Tears rush from her eyes
I want to hold and comfort
But I must say my goodbyes.

"I'm sorry this happened,
But I promise you'll be okay.
I love you and thank you,"
I said as I walked away.

I Once Called To You

"Dear God, Heavenly Father,
Jesus, Your Son and Holy Ghost,
I have my head bowed to You in prayer,
You, whom I was taught to worship most.

I know I am not worthy
To even speak Your name,
But won't You hear a lost sheep's prayer,
Especially one in pain?

I know I am different
In a way that You despise
I suppose You know all this,
Have seen through all my lies.

I've been told I am damned
Like Judas for all time
My soul, licked forever by Inferno's heat,
An eternal agony that is all mine.

I've been told to repent
My ways and turn my soul to You
But I know my nature, dear God above,
So what am I to do?

I've prayed to you,
My God, for years on end,
To save my soul and change me
With each sobbed Amen

I've begged to see Your mercy
To let me hear Your call
To make me in Your straight image
To let me stumble but never fall

For thirty years my prayers unanswered,
My nature still abhorrent to You
Thirty years of tears and pleading
Thirty years of sins accrued

I can't change, God, who I am
How I identify or even love
I've begged to your only Begotten Son
To send intervention from above.

So here I am on my knees,
Making to You my final plea
Help me follow Your straight path
Your Light help me to see.

Amen," I did whisper
No light fell on my shadow long and dark
On my face, I felt a heat
The burn of Lucifer's mark.

And so I turned away
From God's forgiving Light
The harsh brand upon my cheek
Damning me to eternal night.

Nights I Don't Remember, Memories I Can't Forget

Give me the pills and drink
Powder white like snow
Acrid smoke fills my lungs
Who am I? I really don't know.

Euphoria fills my head
Another bump in my nose
Yeah, pass me that cup,
I'll hit that green, which grows.

Pulsing music in my ears
Lights on bodies that writhe
Just give me more,
I feel so alive.

Give me the pills and drink
Powder white like snow
Acrid smoke fills my lungs
Who am I? I really don't know.

In darkness, hands grope
Unwanted I'm so sure,
But give me a hit,
I'm sure I'll want more.

Take the pain away
And the shame when I wake
The bile in my mouth
The mem'ries I did not take

My cheeks are on fire
On the cold tile floor
I don't know what happened
Or what I'm here for.

So give me the pills and drink
Powder white like snow
The question remains
Who am I? The answer: I really don't know.

Turn Straight

A glass of red wine
Innocuous on a bedside table
Crisp white linen sheets on the bed
So I'll sleep if I'm able.

The crashing of a door
I squeeze my eyes tight
If I don't move, perhaps maybe,
He won't rape me tonight.

A heavy weight on the bed
"Whore, I'll turn you straight,"
I close my eyes tighter
This can't be my fate.

The wine glass finally falls
As pain and screams fill the night
A stain of red on white sheets
My very last sight.

Survival

"Baby, don't stop!
Oh my God, yes right there!"
I feel nothing at all
Except his fists in my hair.

The car rocks and shakes
My nose burns, my face numb,
As I try to convince myself
To his passion, I'll succumb.

"I'll call you, I swear,"
He says as he starts the car
"Just drop me off there,
I'll walk, it's not far."

I never know his name
Just swipe right on an app
And just like a magic trick
There's a new guy in my lap.

Some X and cocaine
To get the feeling right
Another guy with empty promises
With whom I can pass the night.

Sometimes in his car
Sometimes in his bed
And like in Miss Saigon,
There's always a movie in my head.

A movie where my life
Unfolds in a different way
One where I can face my own reflection
At the close of each day

One where I don't avoid mirrors
Or hate my own eyes
Because who the hell am I?
I can no longer see through my lies.

Falling Numbers

"Don't eat like that
You're gaining weight
You'll become a whale
No one will date."

"Don't eat like that
We've dances to prepare
Don't you look in the mirror?
You've got a fat roll there."

Slowly it started
Then became a rapid change
Food was the enemy,
Feeling full was a feeling so strange

Numbers filled my head
Calorie counts assaulted my mind
My bones started to show
And people were far more kind.

"No thanks, I'm not hungry."
Another cloaking lie
Another purged meal
Eyes too agonized to cry

Eschew all food
Make love to the scale
See my ugliness in the mirror
My reflection's truth could not fail

Doing lines in the bathroom
Stopped intense hunger pains
I was spiraling out
Of my life, I lost the reins.

But more people liked me
A paragon of beauty, they said
Parading 'round in dresses and heels
My heart and soul lead.

It didn't matter the cost
Of my health, sanity, or life,
I was thin, successful, and popular
So I told myself it was worth all the strife

"But it's all an illusion,
We both know it," an inner voice said
And no matter how I tried
I couldn't get its words from my head.

Terpsichore

Music fills me
Thrills my body and soul
To lose myself in it
Is my only goal

I glide 'round the floor
A waltz plays in my ear
Sweat runs down my brow
Gone is all my fear

My partner and I
Quickstep across the floor
Winning is easy
But I want so much more.

I want to lose myself
In Terpsichore's embrace
To tango with her
Her mark replacing Lucifer's on my face,

Cause when I'm dancing
I am set oh so free
Everything fades away
And I even love me

I feel like I belong
Who I am and what I've done
It it doesn't matter
And I can be Terpsichore's daughter or son.

Sobriety

Sobriety
Twelve years strong.
Sobriety
Only snow in clouds where it belongs
Sobriety
No more hunted and haunted eyes in the glass
Sobriety
Every random drug test I now pass
Sobriety
No more nights forgotten
Sobriety
No more mem'ries I can't forget
Sobriety
Dreams suddenly fulfilled
Sobriety
Nights filled with shame, remorse, and regret
Sobriety
Therapy and rehab
Sobriety
Chips and facilities
Sobriety
Withdrawals that brought me
Sobriety
Down to my knees

Sobriety
The cure worth all the pain
Sobriety
A new life not the same
Sobriety
A clearness deep in my eyes
Sobriety
A stop to the lies
Sobriety
A new strength I never knew I had
Sobriety
Skills to fight the good and the bad
Sobriety
Going twelve years strong
Sobriety
Sober–how I belong.

Creativity

Fingers to keys
Let my thoughts fly top speed
Lose myself in the characters
How they talk and bleed

Write it all out
Get lost in each plot
All of my demons
For a moment, forgot

Words become pages
A new drug in my veins
Creative electricity
Numbs out all my pains

A poetry book published
Plays produced and some read
Those words turn into pages
And bring me back from the dead.

To Dream, To Escape

I'm called a dreamer
With my head in the clouds
A creative blimp floating
A million thoughts echo loud

I love sculpting castles
I build in the sky
The rainbows filled with colors
Never seen by the ord'nary eye

A world I make
Of adventures untold
I'm always the hero
And like Peter Pan, I never grow old

The music I hear
The verses I write
Help me travel the cosmos
And on Falkor take flight

I hear the Little Prince laughing
And Santa's silver bell
Ride hansoms with Holmes
And like Watson, have stories to tell

I've romances and haunts
Create worlds of my own design
Take flight with the Dreamfinder
And Figment I'll find

Swing vines with Tarzan
Fight zombies tooth and nail
In the Hundred-Acre Wood
There's no way to fail

My dreams drive me
In them, I always succeed
I accomplish my goals
And apologies I don't need

The pain disappears
Like smoke from a dragon's flame
All is forgotten
Except for adventurous gain

And in my dreams,
There are moments sublime,
Knowing my own secrets
And conquering worlds that only are mine.

Interlude

"Are you okay?"
My guide's voice cuts through the gloom
"You're breaking through the darkness,
And you're not letting it consume."

"But what else is there?
I see no colors, dull or bright
Is this my life,
Painful, endless, eternal night?"

A soft laugh escapes
The spector I cannot see
"In all darkness there's light,
It needs to glow first to be."

"So I just keep walking
Through this dark forest of pain?
Of mem'ries that assault
And sear soul and brain?"

"It wasn't all dark,
There were glimmers of light,
Keep moving in this direction,
It'll soon grow more bright."

Awakening

A drunken cast party
A whispered voice in my ear,
"Why do you wear makeup,
You're more beautiful, natural, my dear."

Her lips brushed against mine,
My heart and body did thrill
Stars filled my eyes
My soul just couldn't still.

Her arms were soft,
As she held me close,
"This is who you are,"
Whispered some soft inner ghost.

Our bodies entwining in passion
My senses in overdrive
I never once thought I could
Feel so alive.

It lasted only a night
Two bodies sharing pleasure and pain
She left with the light
Her taste and scent still remained.

I heard her car drive off
My heart and mind in a whirl
I knew at once I never felt with a man
What I felt with this girl.

Stasis

Stasis: A period of inactivity
What became of me when she left
My brain completely shut down
My heart and soul fully bereft

I was on autopilot
Hungry and scared
To acknowledge parts of my life
That I wasn't yet prepared

I liked women
I knew this to be true
But family and God would shun me
What the hell was I to do?

A secret relationship
Masquerading as friends
I lost my heart to her
But to stay hidden, there was no amends.

Because of my fear
I lost the girl of my dreams
Changes had to happen
Or I'd unravel at the seams.

How Do You Say…

I'm GAY.
I'M gay.
How the hell do you say
I'm gay?

I love women
Women are for me
No more beds and cars
Of men I hate to see.

I want to shout it,
But I've no idea how,
It's a revelation so big
I need to say it now!

I'm GAY
I'M gay
Hey, here's how you say
I'M GAY!

One Tiny Spark

A new girl every week,
Or so my friends said,
A bit of a Don Juan
Girl here today, tomorrow to me they're dead.

Riley, Christina
Engaged, then goodbye
I couldn't help it
I had this new freedom to try.

Hump 'em and dump 'em
My credo did sing
I'd love them till morning
Then leave when wedding bells threatened to
ring.

This went on for years
Across all the seasons
Ashley and Rae
Here and there without reasons.

"Will you settle down,
Playboy of the Western World?"
But much like in Synge's play
My claims kept getting unfurled.

I did dating apps,
Thought I was one of the greats,
But all of that changed,
When I saw her face.

She had a smile
I'd give my life to see
And her blue eyes
Tamed restless old me.

I knew she deserved better
Than all I'd done
I knew I had to change
Move Heaven, moon, and sun.

She was different
And I can't say why
My heart thrilled with each hello
And died with each goodbye.

Maybe cause she listens
To me when I speak
Or accepts me for me
A writer, poet, designer, teacher, actor, and geek.

Or maybe cause it's when she
Looks at me I can actually see
All that I am
And all I could be.

Whatever the reason
I truly fell in love
And understood for the first time
Why it's a gift from above.

Thoughts

Although I loved women,
And identified as gay,
There was something else in there
Blocking my way

To being happy
To finally being free
Something there in the shadows
That I couldn't quite see.

Child me had the answer
But her words I couldn't recall
How could something so profound
Be with a child so small?

It was something said,
A moment in time,
To recall would free me
From this circling rhyme

That encapsulates my thoughts
That prevents me from sleep
Dear God above, help me
Unlock this hidden secret I keep!

The Darkest Secret Uncovered

A theatre, a building
Where I've been before
An audience taking seats
I certainly know that score.

I'm not backstage,
I didn't write the show,
It's kind of nice going
To support a friend that I know.

The lights start to dim,
His music plays to cheers,
I can't help but smile
As he appears.

I laugh through his first song,
It's fun and it's light
Joy fills me with warmth,
Its glow ever so bright.

His monologue starts
About knowing who he is
And that's when my brain
Starts to churn and whizz.

"In case you didn't know,
I'm gay," he says with a broad smile,
And oh Holy Christ,
My thoughts ran a mile.

How could he do that
Admit who he was so free?
I realized at once
That could never be me.

But why? My brain argued
You're a lesbian, my dear
But all at once I knew
That wasn't quite sincere

All at once, like Icarus
Burned by the sun's hottest flame,
I couldn't say who I was
Because Kelley wasn't my name.

A core memory unlocked
Child me once again did appear
Shaking and trembling
Crying in fear.

"But mom, I'm a boy,"
Child me said, standing in a store
"Like hell you are,
Just shut your mouth and say no more.

God made you a girl
He makes no mistakes
So stop this nonsense
For Jesus Christ's sake!"

My friend was still singing,
His voice a guiding light home
In an audience full of people
I felt utterly alone.

So was that the secret
I kept locked away
That I am a trans man
And not simply gay?

My whole world in an instant
Turned on its ear
And just like child me,
I was shaking in fear.

Who would accept me
At thirty-seven starting a new
But now that the secret was unlocked
What the hell would I do?

I needed to think
I needed to get away
I either needed to fight this
Or accept it some way.

The show ended,
My friend happily appeared,
"You were great," I said
And as he hugged me, I felt his masculine beard.

Suddenly the room closed in again,
And to him I spoke my first and last lie,
"I have to catch a train fast, my friend, but you
rocked it
Goodbye."

Ten blocks away
Could I find my train
But I ran over twenty
To escape my thoughts and pain.

D-A-R-K-N-E-S-S

Darkness
Pills in my hand
Darkness
I formulated a plan
Darkness
A bath running tepid
Darkness
My heart pumping rapid
Darkness
Realizing who I am
Darkness
Knowing I am damned
Darkness
A note I did write
Darkness
I've given up the fight
Darkness
My final goodbye
Darkness
I sit, shake, and cry.
Darkness
My cell phone shatters the gloom
Darkness
A friend calls and not much too soon

Darknes

His voice is soothing and calm

Darknes

He listens closely, a Gilead's Balm

Darkne

"I'm gonna kill myself."

Darkne

"You're not doing that, how can I help?"

Dark

"I'm a trans man," my voice loud in the gloom

Dark

"You can't kill yourself, you're starting to
bloom.

Dar

You're in control, of that I have faith.

Dar

But I have to ask, are you still safe?"

Da

"Yes," I replied, and it was true.

Da

"What's your new name? Kitt? Nice to meet
you.

D

What're your pronouns? With time they evolve.

D

I don't even know mine, it's not a now problem
to solve.

L

This is you, who you're meant to be

Li
You're gonna be all right, you'll soon see
Lig
You know I love you and who you will be
Ligh
And, your new life
Light
Well, I'm so excited to see."

Visibility

"I don't like white walls,"
My Principal did say
"How about a mural by
Your creative GSA?"

I was surprised,
My mouth agape
It was not quite the road
I thought our meeting would take.

My students were so stoked
Their ideas started to flow
"Let's do it about inclusion
And what it means we will show."

Their idea of visibility
Inclusion for everyone
All should be equal
Daughter, in between, and son.

So they started painting flags
Not one LGBTQIA+ group was left out
They created their mascots
"We've got a ton of Pride clout!"

Watching my students work
And seeing the mural's reception
I started to learn
From its conception

True, authentic identity is important
As is being seen
No matter the consequences
Benevolent or mean.

As my students painted,
Inward I did peer
And my own self-acceptance started,
My bloom was starting to appear.

So as white walls turned to rainbows
With each stroke they painted
I was the one who watched
And contemplated.

Kelley or Kitt
Kitt or Kelley
Male or female
Who was I really?

As my Principal praised
And unveiled our mural's theme
I took a deep breath and
Decided to really be seen

So I am Kitt
My authentic self finally revealed
I'm standing here naked,
Nothing more to be concealed.

I am a trans man
Who has been through fire
But now I want to live my way
No longer to myself be a liar.

I continue to write,
To love and to grow,
But I'm mostly excited
To, my own true self, get to know.

The Return

42

Suddenly, I'm standing in colors
Both light and dark
"Does it look different,
From where you did start?"

I saw the glass
But the image was clearer somehow
"Kitt, it's because you're
Looking at who you really are now."

"Who are you really?"
I finally asked my spectral guide,
"I'm the voice of you–Kitt,
Who was, in Kelley, trapped inside."

"When I step through the glass,
Where will I go?"
I felt my guide shrug
"I really don't know.

You've learned all you need
From this Hall of Memory,
What you do with your life,
I'm eager to see.

You did the hardest part
Of this tiring quest
You found yourself,
So ahead do what's best.

Go write a novel,
Poem or play,
Live your life to its fullest
And always seize the day.

Now that you've found yourself
You will go far
And remember to never again
Stifle your own star."

So I stepped through the glass
Colors all seemed to renew
Darkness and light blended,
It seemed as though my spirit grew.

My head quieted
And excitement thrummed in me like a drum
I AM finally Kitt
Ready and waiting for any adventure to come!